MW00856048

DARING TO ACT ON THE TRUTH OF GOD

RISK IT!

DARING TO ACT ON THE TRUTH OF GOD

by Gregg Farah

Illustrated by Scott Angle

A CREATIVE STUDY OF THE BOOK OF ESTHER

Standard Publishing
Cincinnati, Ohio

Table of Contents

All Scripture quotations, unless otherwise indicated, are taken from the HOLY BIBLE, NEW INTERNATIONAL VERSION®. NIV®. Copyright © 1973, 1978, 1984 by International Bible Society. Used by permission of Zondervan Publishing House. All rights reserved.

Cover illustration by Scott Angle
Inside design by Dina Sorn
Edited by Dale Reeves and Leslie Durden

© 1999 by Standard Publishing.
All rights reserved.
Printed in the United States of America.

The Standard Publishing Company,
Cincinnati, Ohio.
A division of Standex International Corporation.

06   05   04   03   02   01   00   99

5   4   3   2   1

ISBN: 0-7847-0951-3

How to Use This Book

Today we have many inaccurate definitions of power:

- The ability to bench-press 300 pounds.
- The ability to intimidate others.
- The ability to get whatever you want.

In his excellent book titled *Esther*, Charles Swindoll provides an accurate description of power: "Unwittingly victimized by an unbearable situation, Esther stepped up and determined, by God's grace, to make a difference. Throwing protocol to the wind and ignoring all her fears, this woman stood in a gap most of her peers would never have risked. In doing so, she not only exposed and foiled the plans of an evil man, who, like Adolph Hitler, had a violent agenda—she alone saved her nation from extermination! Now, that's what I call power!"[1]

Power is not limited to physical strength, nor is it the ability to manipulate others. True biblical power is taking a risk that few CEOs or bodybuilding champions would ever consider. What is that risk? Daring to act on the truth of God!

When we risk doing things God's way, we have enormous power—because it comes from God! And that means that even a 98-pound freshman can successfully lead the biggest, meanest linebacker of a school's football team to Christ. Why? Because true power comes from God. But obtaining this power requires more than hours in a gym. This power demands that you take a risk. What kind of risk?

Consider this true story: Jerome, Rebecca and Vincent stood before me, explaining what life at their school was like: "We're the only Christians in our school. We've tried to get Bible studies going and different outreach events, but as soon as we put up signs to advertise, they either get ripped down or have obscenities written across them. People at our school hate us and hate God."

"What are your plans?" I asked.

"Oh, we're praying and believing that God is going to do unbelievable things this year. And if it isn't this year, then next. And if it's not next year, it's the year after. We believe there's gonna be a revival at this school. And if we graduate before it happens, we know at least we'll have faithfully prayed for it!"

These students dared to act on the truth of God and took a big risk.

F.Y.I.
Who's Who?

Xerxes   Also known as Ahasuerus, the king of Persia.

Vashti   Queen of Persia . . . for a little while at least.

Haman   A wealthy and influential officer to the king. He is second in command to the king . . . for a little while at least.

Mordecai   Esther's cousin, an exiled Jew living in Persia. He serves as a father figure to Esther, having raised her since her parents' deaths.

Esther   Also known as Hadassah, an exiled Jew who becomes queen of Persia after Xerxes demotes Vashti. She is a great example of obedience and faithfulness and risks her life to save her people.

In a Nutshell

Esther's story takes place between chapters 6 and 7 of the book of Ezra, between the first return to Jerusalem led by Zerubbabel and the second return led by Ezra. The book of Esther describes the fate of those Jews who remained in exile in Persia. Mordecai is a descendant of one of those exiled Jews.

TIMELINE

930 B.C.	Civil War—12 tribes of Israel divide. The 10 northern tribes are known as Israel and the two southern tribes are known as Judah.
722 B.C.	Assyria attacks and defeats the northern kingdom, scattering the people. Some tribes migrated south.
586 B.C.	Babylon attacks and defeats the southern kingdom, destroying Jerusalem and exporting the people to Babylon.
537 B.C.	The first return of exiles to Jerusalem under Zerubbabel.
516 B.C.	The temple is completed.
486 B.C.	Ahasuerus (Xerxes I) becomes king of Persia.
479 B.C.	Esther becomes queen.
474 B.C.	Haman's decree to destroy the Jews.
473 B.C.	The first feast of Purim.
458 B.C.	The second return of exiles under Ezra.

Check This . . .
According to the fair use policy, you can legally use multimedia for educational purposes according to these guidelines: you can use a video clip of three minutes or less without securing permission from anyone. If you choose to show more, visit the web site at fairuse.stanford.edu/ for information on whom to contact regarding permission.

They risked their reputations, their friendships and even their physical safety. But they wanted to be part of God's plan—they didn't want to risk missing that!

Esther was a woman of God who risked her life to do what was right and, ultimately, to save her people, the Jews, from extermination. This book is designed to help your students live such a meaningful, daring life. Each session is divided into three sections: **Count the Cost, Get the Truth** and **Take the Risk.** Each of these sections contains more than one option or activity for you to use, depending on available resources and the needs of your students. As you prepare to teach, tailor the lesson to fit your group's learning style and focus on the topic your students most need to learn about. In addition, each session also includes a midweek devotional called **Risky Business.** The devotional continues the theme from the session and challenges students to take a risk for God outside the church's four walls.

The **Count the Cost** section creatively introduces the topic with two options, one of which is more active than the other. This is where a student needs to be hooked! Carefully consider which option would work best for your students and make the necessary adaptations to ensure a great start.

In the **Get the Truth** section, students interact with the Bible—sometimes using reproducible student sheets—in order to see the relevancy between Esther's situation and their own. Again, two options are provided, with one being more active than the other.

Finally, in the **Take the Risk** section, students are challenged to do just that! Both options dare the students to act on the truth of God. At the conclusion of each study, be sure to distribute copies of the reproducible midweek devotional guide, **Risky Business,** to encourage your teenagers to dig into God's Word during the week.

Since the media (especially music and film) make up a large part of students' identities and often shape their culture, each session features **Check This** suggestions for using music and movie clips that reinforce the point you are trying to make. A warning about these suggestions, especially those involving secular media: preview them first! They are not meant to stand by themselves, but to be woven into your presentation of the material. Without proper explanation before or after, they will become merely entertainment and not a teaching tool. Standard Publishing does not necessarily endorse the entire contents of a particular album or movie.

Get set for a great adventure. Esther is an unusual Bible book in that there is no obvious mention of God or reference to faith. But, just as God works mysteriously and sometimes indirectly in our lives, so he creatively makes himself known throughout the book of Esther. There is no mistaking his presence in this book—may the same be true of our students!

Trading Places 1

Are you ready for God to use you? Sometimes God surprises us by giving us opportunities to serve him that we would never expect—so we'd better be ready. This happened to Esther. In chapters 1 and 2, she becomes queen under some pretty interesting circumstances. While it's her beauty that captures the king's eye, it's her heart that enables God to use her. The fact that Esther feared God and honored him kept her available to serve him in any situation. Chapters 1 and 2 also introduce us to Mordecai and Haman, two people whom God used in radically different ways. Are you ready for God to use you? Read on to see how that question changed a nation.

QUESTION OF THE DAY

Make copies of the question below and hand to students as they walk in. The only instruction given to them should be, **"Read it and think about it."**

True or False? God can use you to do amazing things today!

Why do you think that? (Hold that thought! We'll discuss your response later.)

COUNT THE COST

1 ALL DRESSED UP

You'll need to obtain some wild and crazy garb from a thrift store ahead of time. To begin this activity, ask for two to four pairs of volunteers (depending on the size of your group). Choose one person of each pair to be the "model" and the other to be the "coach." Try to have equal guys and girls, but it's not essential. If you do have guys/girls, have the guy be the "model" and the girl the "coach."

Begin this activity by saying, **"Since (*name an upcoming event or holiday*) is coming up, I thought it would be good to get a head start on how to look your best by doing some training. The first element of our training is *preparation*. It is essential that we be quick to prepare for the evening festivities. The best way to do**

LESSON TEXT
Esther 1, 2

LESSON FOCUS
Be ready for God to use you.

LESSON GOALS
As a result of participating in this lesson, students will:

- Compare God's requirements for leaders versus man's.
- Realize God can use them in any and every situation.
- Evaluate the condition of their hearts to see if they're really ready for God to use them.

Materials needed:
Makeup or face paint for two to four volunteers; plenty of towels for cleanup; tarp to cover the floor; large table or a desk and a chair for each volunteer; equal amount of assorted clothes for each volunteer

that is to practice."

Have partners stand next to each other with an equal amount of clothing at their feet. Divide your group evenly so that everyone is cheering for a pair. On "go," the coach is to dress the model as quickly as possible. The model is not allowed to use his hands to help in any way. The first model to get all clothes on is the winner.

Comment, **"The second element of our training is *presentation*. We need to look our best and that means getting help from a coach. Since speed is important, we will see who looks best after a 20-second makeup session."**

Have each model sit in the chair with his hands behind his back and his coach kneeling behind him. On "go," each coach must put makeup (or face paint) on the model by reaching around him. The coach should not be able to see what she is doing! (Make sure the models have something to completely cover their clothes and that they keep their eyes closed.)

Continue by saying, **"Finally, *personality* is critical. It is important that we be in a good mood during this celebration. So we will have our models, one at a time, walk in front of you in order to demonstrate their charm and confidence."**

Have each model walk across the room and back. Have students who are watching score each contestant by writing down numbers (1-10) and holding them up or by holding up a score on their fingers. (Don't worry about the score; we're just keeping everyone involved!) After all models have paraded, have students applaud them and let them leave to get washed up.

Conclude by saying, **"We may laugh at this display of beauty, but believe it or not God used a beauty pageant to help save an entire nation. We'll discover how throughout our study of Esther, but today let's see how it all got started."**

MADE TO ORDER

Begin this activity by asking, **"Who is 100% satisfied with the job our President is doing? What would you change about this person? Today, each of us is responsible for creating the ideal person to be president."**

Form groups of three to six students, then instruct groups to choose one person to lie down on the newsprint and trace his or her outline. Next, each group should brainstorm qualities and characteristics of the ideal person to elect to the presidency. Encourage them to think about the entire person: what the person looks like, his or her character, intellect, hobbies, wardrobe, etc. Encourage students to be as specific as possible. As they mention these characteristics, they should fill in the body outline with the different characteristics they mention. After five minutes, have each group hang up its picture and describe its creation to the other groups.

After students have taped their creations to the wall, discuss these questions:

Check This . . .
Be sure to have a camera or video camera on hand—you'll probably capture some memorable footage!

Materials needed:
About 8 feet of newsprint for each group; markers; masking tape

Check This . . .
Take a picture of each group posing in front of its poster.

- **What similarities are found on the different posters?**
- **What is unique to another group's poster that you really like?**
- **Are looks or abilities emphasized more on all the posters? Why do you think it ended up that way?**
- **Which characteristic on your poster do you think God is most interested in? Why?**

Conclude this activity by saying, **"Sometimes God surprises us in how he intends to use us. Today we're beginning a study on Esther, a woman who became queen of an entire nation. We'll find out if her characteristics match those you came up with, and we'll also find out if she had anything to offer. And in doing so, maybe we'll find out if you have more to offer God than you think."**

GET THE TRUTH

1 ON TRIAL!

Introduce the activity by asking, **"What do you think is God's attitude towards beauty pageants? Why?** (Give time for student response.) **Let's find out how he used one to select a queen who loved him."**

Form groups of three to six students and give each group one of the assignments from the "On Trial!" student sheet. (If you have more than four groups, you can give more than one group the same assignment.) Inform them they will have about ten minutes to compile their information. Then allow each group to report and groups 1 and 2 to debate. Instruct the storytellers from each group to go first so that everyone knows the flow of the two chapters. Then have groups 3 and 4 share their discoveries first and have them decide the victor of the debate between groups 1 and 2.

Comment, **"Regardless of what you think about King Xerxes, God allowed him to choose a new queen by holding a beauty pageant. Esther never planned on being queen, yet she rose to a position of great authority. What about you? Are you prepared for God to use you in an unexpected way?"**

2 PICKING UP THE PIECES

Form groups of three to five, possibly by allowing students to select the winner in a "You're So Ugly, You're Cute" pet pageant. Bring in several pet photos from kids' magazines for them to "judge." Students who choose the same pet will be in the same group for this activity. Distribute copies of the student sheet located on page 15 of this book.

Introduce this activity by saying, **"When you spend time looking at someone else and evaluating him or her, you can't help but look at yourself. Do you ever wish you were someone else? Ever feel like life could be so much better under different circumstances? In your small groups, read through 'Picking Up the Pieces' and discuss the questions at the end. Then we'll compare that scenario with a simi-**

Check This . . .
Another option is to play "Beautiful You," recorded by Considering Lily on their CD by the same name or "Picture Perfect," by Michael W. Smith on his *Change Your World* album. Discuss what the song says about "true beauty." Ask if they agree or disagree. Or play the song while the groups are working.

Materials needed:
Bibles; writing utensils; reproducible student sheet on page 14 of this book

Materials needed:
Bibles; writing utensils; pet photos; reproducible student sheet on page 15 of this book

Check This . . .
To help remind students to trust God during tough times, listen to "In the Name," recorded by Jennifer Knapp on her *Kansas* CD.

lar Bible story that deals with life's crazy times."

Allow time for students to read and consider both the bad day scenario and Esther's situation. Then conclude by saying, **"Esther became queen under some pretty interesting circumstances. She may have been selected because of her beauty, but the condition of her heart determined whether or not God could use her. God also wants to use you wherever he has allowed you to be. The question is, are you ready to used by God? If he gives you a unique opportunity to serve him, how will you respond?"**

TAKE THE RISK

1 GETTIN' READY

Materials needed:
Overhead projector, overhead projector transparency and marker; or chalkboard and chalk

Refer to the "Question of the Day" distributed at the beginning of the session. Comment, **"Remember the slip of paper you were handed when you arrived today? What's your response to the true/false statement: 'God can use you to do amazing things today!'?"** (Allow time for student response.)

Discuss the following questions, listing answers to the first two on the board or overhead for all to see:

- **Why do you think God allowed Esther to be chosen as queen?** (Challenge students to go beyond her beauty.)
- **What other qualities is God looking for in a person's life in order to be able to serve him?**
- **Why are these qualities important?**

Check This . . .
Be patient! If students do not answer right away, wait! Wait at least 20 seconds, and then ask again. If necessary, call on someone (maybe another leader first, and then a student, or better yet—volunteer your response!). Don't forget to follow up their responses with a probing "Why?"

Instruct students to gather in their original groups so each person can share his or her answer to the following two questions:

- **Which of the qualities mentioned do you feel is one of your strengths?**
- **Which of these qualities do you need help with?**

Then have group members pray that God would help them further develop the areas they are strong in and/or help them in the areas they are weak.

2 YOUR EKG

Materials needed:
Paper; writing utensils; overhead projector, transparency and marker or chalkboard and chalk; reproducible student sheet on page 16 of this book

Ahead of time, you will need to prepare an overhead transparency which pictures a large heart with the words from Romans 5:1 written inside: "Therefore, since we have been justified through faith, we have peace with God through our Lord Jesus Christ."

Begin this activity by referring to the "Question of the Day" distributed at the beginning of the session. Ask, **"Remember the slip of paper you were handed when you arrived today? What's your response to the true/false statement: 'God can use you to do amazing things today!'?"** (Allow time for student response.)

Pass out paper and writing utensils. Instruct each person to draw a giant heart that will fill up his or her paper as you say, **"God allowed Esther to be queen for a reason, and he allows our lives to go a certain way for a reason, too. Whether we play on a team, work at** a job or simply go to school as a student, God wants to use us in great ways. But it's the condition of our heart that determines whether or not we will be used.

"Think of two qualities in a person's life that God is looking for. Write those qualities down inside the heart on your paper. Take 30 seconds to write down as many more qualities you can think of that God is looking for in each of our lives."

After 30 seconds, have students share their answers. Comment, **"We've just shown what a healthy heart looks like."** (Read all responses that have been gathered.) Continue, **"But does this reflect the condition of your heart? I can honestly say I'm weak in these areas:** (share which ones). **What about you? If this is what a healthy heart looks like** (show a piece of clean, unwrinkled paper), **then fold or crumple your paper to identify the condition of your own heart."** (Give students time to do this.)

Then say, **"If we are honest, all of us probably feel like our paper should be ripped to shreds. Too often we all fall short of what God desires. But remember God can and wants to perfectly heal each of our hearts. In fact, if you're a Christian, he has healed your heart."** (Show overhead transparency of the Romans 5:1 heart.) **"Now we need to live the way God has enabled us to. Let's take time to thank God for the new heart he has given us and the ability to live for him right where we are."**

Close in prayer and distribute copies of **Risky Business**, the mid-week devotional found on page 16, to each student.

Check This . . .
Be sure to do the same on the board or overhead. Write student responses in as they share them.

Check This . . .
Encourage students who are not Christians to talk to you or privately approach them and ask, "How's your heart?"

ON TRIAL!

Group 1

You represent King Xerxes.
Read Esther 1.

Roles for Group 1:
Storyteller – Retell the events of the chapter.
Half of the group – Defend the king! Think about what accusations can be made against your client and prepare a defense.
Half of the group – Prosecute the queen! Think about ways you can prove she's at fault.

Group 2

You represent Queen Vashti.
Read Esther 1.

Roles for Group 2:
Storyteller – Retell the events of the chapter.
Half of the group – Defend the queen! Think about what accusations can be made against your client and prepare a defense.
Half of the group – Prosecute the king! Think about ways you can prove he's at fault.

Group 3

You represent Mordecai.
Read Esther 2.

Roles for Group 3:
Storyteller – Retell the events of the chapter.
The rest of the group – First, list as many things as you can about Mordecai; then write down as many song titles, TV shows or movie titles you can think of that reflect his character.

Group 4

You represent Esther.
Read Esther 2.

Roles for Group 4:
Storyteller – Retell the events of the chapter.
The rest of the group – First, list as many things as you can about Esther; then make a list of what characters from any books, TV shows or movies you think she resembles.

  ©1999 by The Standard Publishing Company. Permission is granted to reproduce this page for ministry purposes only—not for resale.

PICKING UP THE PIECES

All day long you've been picking up the pieces. What do I mean? Check this out:

Just before lunch your teacher tells you that your lab partner has been suspended for the next two weeks. Your project is due in two days and all that's left is the half of the project your partner was *supposed* to do. You're left with her mess.

Your team goes into the last inning leading by three runs. The pitcher hits the first batter and walks the next two. The bases are loaded with no outs and the coach wants you to pitch. You're left with the other guy's mess.

As you're walking towards your home, you can hear your parents yelling at one another—again. This was supposed to be the night they took you out to celebrate your birthday. Your dad walks by you without saying a word. He slams the car door and drives off and, once again, you're left with a mess.

Discuss with your group:

• **When you finally make it to your room and look back on your day, what thoughts come to your mind?**

• **Could God have used you in any of these situations? How?**

Compare your bad day with this historic "bad day." Read chapter 1 of Esther, then discuss these questions:

• **What are some things (positive or negative) people could say about King Xerxes? About Queen Vashti?**

• **How would you change the advice given to the king?**

Read chapter 2 of Esther, then discuss:

• **List seven things you discover about Esther.**

• **Describe how Esther may have felt when she was chosen to be queen. (Remember the circumstances!)**

©1999 by The Standard Publishing Company. Permission is granted to reproduce this page for ministry purposes only—not for resale.

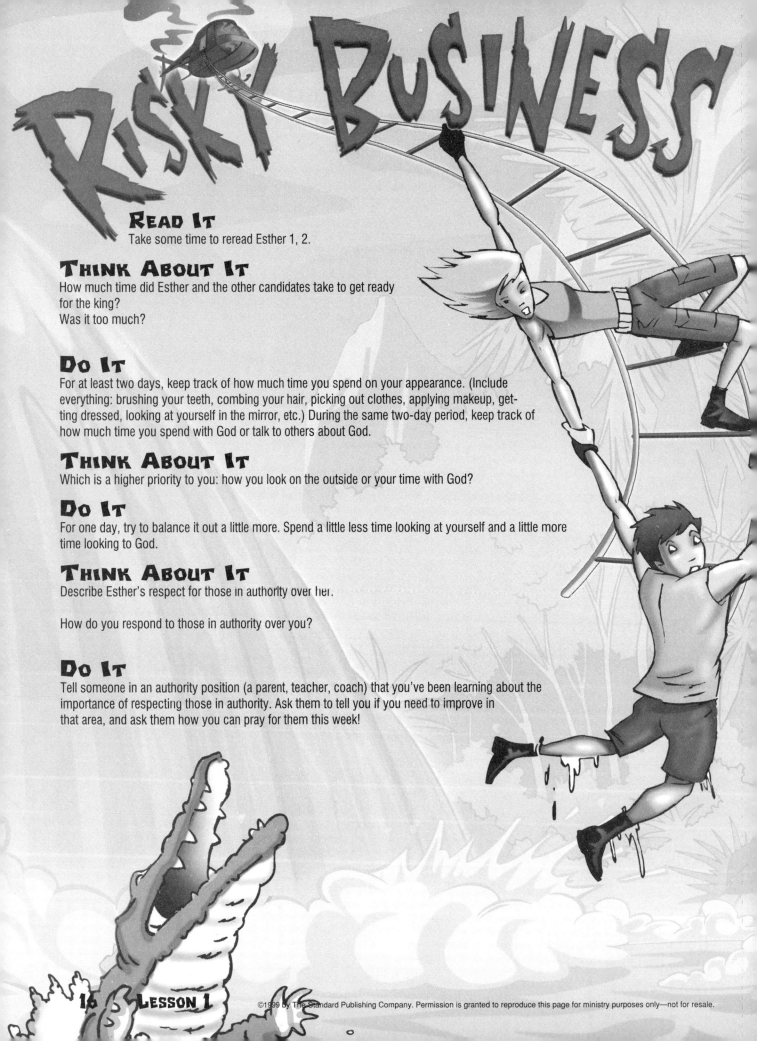

RISKY BUSINESS

READ IT
Take some time to reread Esther 1, 2.

THINK ABOUT IT
How much time did Esther and the other candidates take to get ready for the king?
Was it too much?

DO IT
For at least two days, keep track of how much time you spend on your appearance. (Include everything: brushing your teeth, combing your hair, picking out clothes, applying makeup, getting dressed, looking at yourself in the mirror, etc.) During the same two-day period, keep track of how much time you spend with God or talk to others about God.

THINK ABOUT IT
Which is a higher priority to you: how you look on the outside or your time with God?

DO IT
For one day, try to balance it out a little more. Spend a little less time looking at yourself and a little more time looking to God.

THINK ABOUT IT
Describe Esther's respect for those in authority over her.

How do you respond to those in authority over you?

DO IT
Tell someone in an authority position (a parent, teacher, coach) that you've been learning about the importance of respecting those in authority. Ask them to tell you if you need to improve in that area, and ask them how you can pray for them this week!

©1999 by The Standard Publishing Company. Permission is granted to reproduce this page for ministry purposes only—not for resale.

Lethal Labels 2

"I hate *those* people. They bug me. I wish they'd leave or move or something." Ever hear someone talk like that? An attitude like that is often the result of a single negative encounter with a person—or group of people. Instead of seeking to understand the person or clarify a misunderstanding, the easy response is hatred and retaliation. And that hatred usually extends beyond the individual to any person that looks or acts like them. Labels aren't just about a person's ethnic background. People are also labeled because of their personality traits, interests, looks, abilities—just about anything! In Esther 3, the lives of thousands of Jewish people were in jeopardy because of one man's (Haman's) misunderstanding of another man's (Mordecai's) action. How do you respond in a situation like that? Or how should you not respond when tension between groups of people seems out of control? You're about to find out.

COUNT THE COST

GOTTA SEE IT TO BELIEVE IT

Begin this activity by saying, **"Think of a group of people at school or in your neighborhood that are considered 'different.' Why are they considered different? Do you think everyone in that group has those characteristics? Is there anything wrong with those characteristics?"**

Continue by asking, **"Has someone ever labeled you? Sometimes labels are nice: 'He's smart, talented, friendly, a good listener,' etc. Other times, labels hurt—they can be considered lethal: 'She's stupid, fat, gross.' People are labeled in different ways. The easiest way is by how they look, but lots of times people get labeled because of what they believe, what music they like or what friends they have. Let's take a look at a video clip [or listen to a song] that labels people and consider the negative power of that label."**

Show a three-minute clip from one of these two movies: "The

LESSON TEXT
Esther 3

LESSON FOCUS
Check your labels: your pride and prejudice are showing.

LESSON GOALS
As a result of participating in this lesson, students will:
• Evaluate why people label other people.
• Understand the power and potential of hatred.
• Write an action plan they can use to counter stereotypes.
• Commit to be part of the solution rather than the problem.

Materials needed:
Selected CD or video; TV and VCR or CD player

Hiding Place" or "Schindler's List." Choose a scene that emphasizes racial tension or the effects of someone being labeled. Other video clips you can show are "From the Top," from *Edge TV*, vol. 18; "Racism: Going Color Blind," from *Total TV Network*; or "Teenagers in the KKK," from *Group Talk Starter*, vol. 1.

If you choose to go with a song, some that would work well include "Colored People," recorded by dc Talk on their album *Jesus Freak*; or "Banneryear," by Five Iron Frenzy on their release *Our Newest Album Ever*.

After watching the video clip or listening to the song, discuss the following:

- **In what ways did we see someone labeled?**
- **What messages did those labels carry?**
- **Do you know someone who has been labeled?**
- **What happened and how did they deal with it?**

Close by saying, **"Being labeled can hurt. Because people often use labels negatively, labels can be considered lethal. Let's take a look in Esther 3 at a guy named Haman and how his hatred for another man got out of control."**

WHAT DO YOU DO?

Divide students into groups of three to five, then say, **"Consider what you would do about the following dilemma: Your good friend is running for class president against someone you have always admired but don't really know. You've admired this person because he works hard, stays out of trouble and seems to handle himself with a lot more maturity than most of the people in your class. He's certainly not popular, but that's because he doesn't go out of his way to show off or anything.**

"On the day of the campaign speech, your friend boasts about making school more fun, easier and having lots more school dances. His opponent talks about discipline, hard work and making a difference that will positively impact the community. Your friend expects you to vote for him, but you think it would be wiser to vote for his opponent."

Give groups about five minutes to discuss the following questions:

- **What issues are at stake?**
- **What advantages are there if you vote for your friend? What disadvantages?**
- **What advantages are there if you vote for his opponent? What disadvantages?**
- **What do you do?**

Comment, **"Showing favoritism is dangerous, and God tells us not to play favorites (James 2:1-4). But we're often guilty. What are some possible consequences to playing favorites?"** (Discuss as a group.) **"One problem with showing favorites is that it's a sign of selfishness and pride. We pick certain people or do certain things because they benefit us. In Esther 3, we see an exam-**

ple of how selfishness and pride can turn deadly. They can powerfully influence us to do foolish things. Let's take a closer look."

GET THE TRUTH

JUST THE FACTS

Briefly review the situation in which Esther found herself in chapters 1 and 2 to set the scene. To help the review, you may want to have students play the roles of the main characters from chapters 1 and 2 and act out the story.

Write the words **"Who? Where? What? Why?"** on the board and discuss the answers to those questions as you read through chapter 3 in three sections:

Section 1:   Esther 3:1-6
Section 2:   Esther 3:7-11
Section 3:   Esther 3:12-15

Be sure to get a response from each question to ensure understanding. You may need to clarify who the characters are. (See the "Who's Who?" list on page 7.) Racist attitudes and stereotypes are a significant factor in this chapter. Challenge your students throughout the discussion to consider modern parallels.

Comment, **"Unfortunately the events from Esther 3 happen far too often in our world today. What are some modern-day examples of people being stereotyped and wrongly labeled?"**

Brainstorm two or three examples as a large group. Then divide students into small groups of about three to six and have them brainstorm at least two additional modern examples. Then have them pick their favorite example to act out in front of the other groups. Instruct them that the example they choose has to relate in some way to the events from Esther 3. Allow as many groups to perform as time allows.

Conclude this activity by saying, **"Esther provides one example of the negative power of labeling others. And you've presented some additional modern-day insights! But let's see if there's a way out of this mess."**

THEN AND NOW

Distribute writing utensils and copies of the student sheet on page 22 of this book to your students. Then say, **"The Bible is not some ancient boring book! It's God's Word that helps us know how to live today. It also provides examples (good and bad) that we can learn from. Work through the following assignment that looks at a situation from 'then' and how it applies to a situation you're in 'now.'"**

Split students into groups of three or four and direct them to work through the student sheet together. After 10 minutes, bring students back as a big group and let a spokesperson from each group share their discoveries.

Materials needed:
Bibles; paper; writing utensils; chalkboard or dry-erase board; chalk or marker

Materials needed:
Bibles; reproducible student sheet on page 22 of this book; writing utensils

Then say something like this: **"It's good to look at the past so we can learn and grow from it for the future. Now let's focus on ways we can be sure to defeat the problem of labeling others today!"**

TAKE THE RISK

1 PLAYBACK

Ask students, **"Why do people label others?"** (Allow time for them to respond. Possible answers might include *pride, self-ishness, arrogance, prejudice, insecurity* or *their upbringing*.) Continue by saying, **"Anytime someone looks down on someone else, it's because they think they are better than the other person. The Bible says we should have exactly the opposite attitude."** (Read Philippians 2:3, 4.)

Comment, **"But reality reveals that we're often labeled unfairly. So what do we do when that happens? What's an appropriate Christian response?"**

Brainstorm as a large group different Christian ways to respond to stereotypes. For example, how can Mordecai respond to Haman in this situation? Or use one or more of the student examples from the previous activity. Come up with a list of five to ten appropriate responses and write them on the board.

Hand out writing utensils and copies of the student sheet on page 23. After giving students time to work through the sheet, discuss questions they may have and give them an opportunity to share their insights. Then close in prayer, asking God to give each one the courage to apply his truth in tough situations and the courage to make things right with others.

2 TODAY'S TOP 10

Introduce this activity by saying, **"There are hundreds of reasons that would explain *why* people label others. Right now I'm looking for only about twenty. How many of you can think of at least one reason other people are labeled or stereotyped?"** (Wait for hands! Once you have at least three or four hands raised, continue.) **"As soon as you can think of one, come and write it on the board."** Invite students to write their responses on the board and continue encouraging them until you have about twenty written down.

Once students have completed this task, continue, **"Now we want to come up with our own 'Top 10' list. Let's eliminate reasons until there are only the top 10 reasons remaining."**

Comment, **"We don't want to just identify the problem, we want to come up with some solutions! With the person next to you, try to come up with what you think would be the 'Top 3' solutions to this problem. Number them in what you consider the order of priority."** (Number 1 would be the top answer and number 3 would be the third best answer.)

Give students a chance to share responses by listening to several

Materials needed:
Bibles; reproducible student sheet on page 23 of this book; writing utensils; dry-erase board or chalkboard; marker or chalk

Check This . . .
Students may find this difficult! Too often they don't believe the Bible provides direction to real-life situations. Jump-start them with ideas, but don't do the whole activity for them—make them think!

Some resource ideas that list Bible verses topically (such as pride and self-centeredness) are:

The A to Z Guide to Bible Application (Tyndale); *The Handbook of Bible Application* (Tyndale); *Armed and Dangerous: Straight Answers from the Bible*, by Ken Abraham (Barbour Books); and *The Contemporary Concordance of Bible Topics*, by Ken Anderson (Victor Books).

Materials needed:
Reproducible student sheet on page 24 of this book; dry-erase board or chalkboard; marker or chalk

Check This . . .
For added interest, play a tape of a drum-roll similar to David Letterman's Top 10 countdown.

number 3 responses, then number 2 and finally number 1.

Close by saying, **"Consider which one of these solutions you need to apply this week. I encourage you to take a risk this week by committing to beating the labeling game. Decide that you aren't going to play that game anymore. I look forward to hearing about your strategies and successes next week."**

Lead students in prayer for the courage to love rather than label others. Distribute copies of **Risky Business**, the midweek devotional found on page 24, as your students depart.

One of the reasons we study the Bible is to know how we should live. As we look at some events that took place "then," we can see how they apply to us "now." Read chapter 3 of Esther as a group and then work through the following questions together.

THEN

Look at Esther 3 and list anything you know about each main character:

• King Xerxes

• Haman

• Mordecai

• What problem does chapter 3 identify?

• Why does the problem exist?

• What do you think God wants to accomplish?

NOW

Compare this problem from Esther to a modern-day problem.

• How are the characters similar or dissimilar?

• What is the modern-day solution?

• What do we learn about God from the modern-day situation?

 ©1999 by The Standard Publishing Company. Permission is granted to reproduce this page for ministry purposes only—not for resale.

PLAYBACK

We have the potential to learn a lot from our past if we take the time to do it. Want a chance to grow? Work through these four steps.

STEP 1

We've seen one example from Esther of the negative effects the Jewish people experienced from being labeled based on one man's misunderstanding of another man's actions. You also thought of some others in your small group. Now I want you to think of a time *you* were unfairly labeled, a time when someone called you something that was not true. Write a brief description of how that incident ended (your feelings, your relationship with that person or group, etc.).

STEP 2

If you could go back and relive that situation, what would you do? There are lots of bad ways to handle the situation, but let's consider some of the Christlike responses we just discussed. Pick three ideas from our "Top 10" list that could have worked in your situation.

STEP 3

There's no guarantee that your situation will change if you obey God. But when you obey God, *you* always change. Write down a couple of ways you might change if you applied those three ideas.

STEP 4

Are you guilty of unfairly labeling someone? If so, plan when you will apologize to God and that person.

©1999 by The Standard Publishing Company. Permission is granted to reproduce this page for ministry purposes only—not for resale.

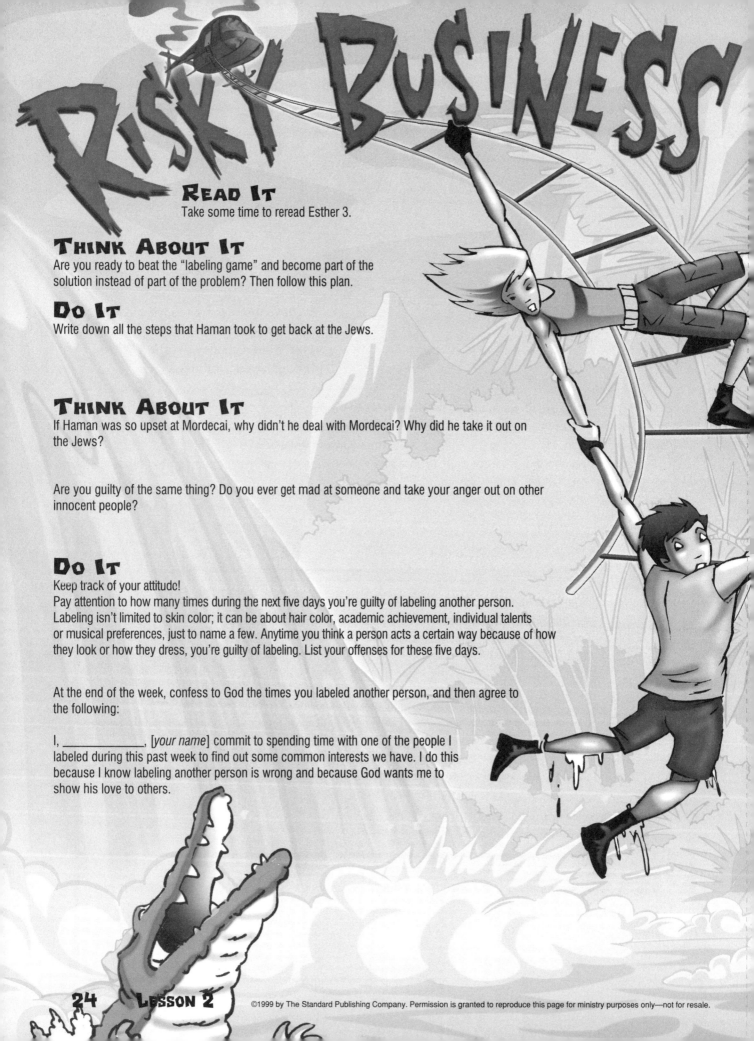

RISKY BUSINESS

READ IT
Take some time to reread Esther 3.

THINK ABOUT IT
Are you ready to beat the "labeling game" and become part of the solution instead of part of the problem? Then follow this plan.

DO IT
Write down all the steps that Haman took to get back at the Jews.

THINK ABOUT IT
If Haman was so upset at Mordecai, why didn't he deal with Mordecai? Why did he take it out on the Jews?

Are you guilty of the same thing? Do you ever get mad at someone and take your anger out on other innocent people?

DO IT
Keep track of your attitude!
Pay attention to how many times during the next five days you're guilty of labeling another person. Labeling isn't limited to skin color; it can be about hair color, academic achievement, individual talents or musical preferences, just to name a few. Anytime you think a person acts a certain way because of how they look or how they dress, you're guilty of labeling. List your offenses for these five days.

At the end of the week, confess to God the times you labeled another person, and then agree to the following:

I, _____, [your name] commit to spending time with one of the people I labeled during this past week to find out some common interests we have. I do this because I know labeling another person is wrong and because God wants me to show his love to others.

©1999 by The Standard Publishing Company. Permission is granted to reproduce this page for ministry purposes only—not for resale.

THAT'S NOTHING!

Regardless of which option you choose for this section, you will need to begin with this activity, as both options build on it.

As students arrive, direct them to a table that has slips of paper, writing utensils and a shoe box (or some container for collecting the papers). Each paper should be titled, "That's Nothing!" with the following instruction:

What's the worst possible thing that could happen to someone your age? (Describe in detail.) (A prize will be awarded to the writer of the most creative response, so be sure to sign your name!)

After students fill out the paper, have them drop it in the box and then allow them to mingle until you officially begin.

COUNT THE COST

1 DOOMSDAY DISCOVERY

Before class, draw a target on the board (like a dartboard) composed of five circles with the smallest, circle #1, being the bull's-eye. The circles, moving from the outside in, should have the following phrases written on them:

Circle #5: **You're grounded for two weeks.**

Circle #4: **Your brother records your phone conversations and sells the tape at your school dance.**

Circle #3: **Everyone at school is laughing at you because of a rumor about you.**

Circle #2: **You and your family get in a major car accident.**

Circle #1: **Your best friend gets cancer.**

To begin, divide students into five groups. (One person can be a group.)

Say, **"Life happens! Every day something crazy happens that impacts us in a significant or minor way. Often we have no control over what impacts us, but we always have control over how we respond.**

Materials needed:
Copies of "That's Nothing!" strips of paper; a shoe box or hat; writing utensils; prize

LESSON TEXT
Esther 4

LESSON FOCUS
Pray—don't pout or panic—when faced with problems.

LESSON GOALS
As a result of participating in this lesson, students will:

- Consider how their responses to life's situations reveal their true faith in God.
- Realize that God is in control of where they are in life and that they have control over their attitudes.
- Evaluate whether they pout or pray when confronted with problems.
- Commit to making a difference in the lives of those around them.

Materials needed:
Five copies of a picture of a piece of burning dynamite you have drawn (or use candles); masking tape; five blindfolds; dry-erase board or chalkboard; marker or chalk

Check This . . .
A song that recounts the story of Esther is "Who God Is Gonna Use," recorded by the late Rich Mullins on his album *The World as Best as I Can Remember It: Volume One.*

Check This . . .
Be sure to play music while they are doing this, perhaps a depressing song that talks about misery. Some possibilities might be a country-western or blues song.

Materials needed:
The "That's Nothing!" box

Check This . . .
Be careful about how long you allow the students to ad lib. Some students shine in this environment but others get intimidated. A good rule of thumb is to stop the scene while things are going well—keep the audience wanting more! (And protect your students from bombing in front of their peers!)

Check This . . .
After your discussion, pull out a couple more "That's Nothing!" slips and give a prize to the writer of the most creative response.

"I'm going to place you into groups and your group is about to be impacted. Most of us have played the game 'Pin the Tail on the Donkey.' Today, we're going to use that same idea and play 'Doomsday Discovery.' Each group will send one brave volunteer to the board to determine the fate of his or her group. After your group's fate is discovered, you may keep your discovery or trade it in for a new one from the 'That's Nothing!' box."

Blindfold the five volunteers and give them each a piece of "dynamite" with a piece of masking tape on it. Then, spin them around and ask them to go choose their fate. Dynamite should be numbered or marked in some way to identify each group.

If the target is large enough, send everyone at the same time to speed things up and to add confusion. Instruct students that any selections made outside of the target area require you to select a slip from the "That's Nothing!" box used in the opening activity. After selections are made, do your best "Let's make a deal" imitation to entice groups to trade their "Doomsday Discovery" for a selection from the "That's Nothing!" box.

After each group's fate has been determined, randomly read selections from the "That's Nothing!" box and reward a prize to the writer of the most original idea. (Keep track of time—don't spend the entire lesson doing this!)

Conclude this activity by saying, **"Sometimes life is like 'Doomsday Discovery.' We never intend for something bad to happen, but when it does, we're stuck with it. How we respond to our situation reveals a lot about our character and even more about our faith in God. Today we're going back to the book of Esther to see how she and Mordecai responded when their lives and all of their relatives' lives were in jeopardy."**

POUT OR PRAY?

Ask for two volunteers and pull out a piece of paper from the "That's Nothing!" box to read aloud to the students. Before reading, inform everyone that these two students will continue the story that was just read. However, they can respond in only one of two ways: they can pout or pray.

After reading, ask the group, **"Do you want them to 'pout or pray'?"** Invite students to shout out their responses. If "pout" is selected, the students must continue the story by expressing a completely negative attitude. If "pray" is selected, the students will continue with a positive attitude, because they know and believe that God is in control. After several pairs of volunteers have participated, discuss the following questions:

- **In what ways did their attitude affect their situation?**
- **Can you think of a real example from your life when your perspective made all the difference?**
- **When bad things happen, is it easier to pout or to pray? Why is that?**

• **What makes it easier to pray and keep a godly perspective?**

Say, **"Attitude is everything! If you claim to be a Christian, you have to trust that God is in control, even during tough times. How you respond to your situation reflects how God can use you and what he can teach you. Let's look at two people from Esther who faced a situation that challenged their trust in God."**

GET THE TRUTH

① CAN OF WORMS

Read Esther 4 aloud as a group. Lead a brief discussion about what's happening while answering any questions. Be sure to discuss the different ways the characters could have responded. Ask the following questions to get the discussion rolling:

VERSES 1-8

• **Why is Mordecai so upset?**
• **What's the difference between whining and communicating real emotional hurt? Which is Mordecai doing?**
• **When have you been so upset it made you feel sick?**

VERSES 9-17

• **Since Esther is queen, why can't she just walk up to the king and talk to him?**
• **What is Mordecai's response in verses 13 and 14 to Esther's reservations?**
• **Has there ever been a time in your life when you were the perfect person for the job, a time when only you could complete the task? How did that make you feel?**
• **What is Esther's final plan? What other options did she and Mordecai have?**

Continue by saying, **"Esther and Mordecai are faced with a life-and-death situation. Not all of us have to deal with that kind of pressure, but we all face challenging times that make us wonder where God is and what he wants us to do. I'm going to put you into groups and hand each group a can with several different questions in it. The first person in the group is to reach in and grab a question and give an honest response. Then pass the can to the next person and continue until everyone has had a chance. Don't peek at the questions before you choose them!"**

Have students form groups of five or fewer, possibly by choosing their favorite comedian from among five options. (Possible choices include Drew Carey, Jim Carrey, Mike Myers, Chris Rock and Robin Williams.) After students make their selections, you may need to adjust the groups so they are of equal size. Send the groups to different areas of the room and give each group a "can of worms."

Allow five to ten minutes for them to discuss their "worms," then wrap up this activity by concluding, **"All of us are faced with challenging situations, but not all of us respond in the best way. Perspective is one factor that determines our response. Let's take**

Materials needed:
Bibles; writing utensils; several copies of the reproducible student sheet on page 30 of this book (cut into strips); a coffee can or box for each group to discuss responses

Check This . . .
Think of some other worms and toss 'em in the can!

27

a look at how perspective matters."

A MELODRAMA

Inform the students that everyone is going to do some acting but that you need seven volunteers to come up front. Assign the roles and instruct the audience to provide the background set sounds, such as birds chirping or a breeze blowing, and to participate at the appropriate spots while the narrator pauses. Be sure to instruct the narrator to pause while students are acting or the crowd is responding.

The roles you will need are these: narrator, Martin, Estelle, Estelle's friends (3), Hank and the participating audience. Give a copy of the reproducible sheet on page 31 to the narrator and begin the action.

After the melodrama has been presented, thank all the participants and read Esther 4. Then ask the following questions:

- **What's going on?**
- **What is Esther's plan of attack?**
- **What other options can you think of to respond to this situation?**
- **Have you ever been in a situation where something bad would have happened if you hadn't acted? What happened?**

Conclude, **"Not all of us face life-and-death situations like this, but we all deal with challenging circumstances that require us to respond. How we respond reflects whether or not we trust God. Let's look at how Esther 4 applies to our lives."**

TAKE THE RISK

LOOK AT IT THIS WAY . . .

Have students return to their original small groups from the first activity. Instruct them to think back to their "Doomsday Discovery" experience and answer the following questions:

- **What are the negative aspects of the tough times we experience?**
- **What are some potentially positive aspects?**
- **When bad things happen, do you believe God is in control of your life?**
- **If you do, what do you think he might be trying to teach you during those times? If you don't, why not?**
- **Would it matter to you whether or not you knew God was still in control? Why?**
- **If you had a positive attitude, one that continued to trust in God, how would that affect you?**
- **How would a negative attitude affect you?**

Allow about ten minutes for small-group discussion before inquiring, **"Think about your life right now. What is one way your attitude needs to change to show that you're trusting in God?"** Have students pray for one another in their small groups.

Materials needed:
Reproducible student sheet on page 31 of this book; Bibles

Check This . . .
The book of Esther records dramatic high-stakes historical events which warrant more than a monotone recitation. If you are dramatically challenged, recruit a good reader who can add dramatic inflection to the Scripture reading without being melodramatic! Assigning three readers—narrator, Mordecai and Esther—would make the Scripture really come alive.

Materials needed:
Copy of the list of questions for each group

Check This . . .
Two VeggieTale songs that address trusting that God is in control are "God Is Bigger" and "Fear Not, Daniel," both of which are recorded on the *VeggieTunes* CD.

WHAT TIME?

Reread Mordecai's response from Esther 4:13, 14 and then write the words from the end of verse 14 on the board: "'And who knows but that you have come to royal position for such a time as this?'" Distribute paper and writing utensils to students. Then ask, **"When you see and hear this verse, what comes to mind? Take the next two minutes to write or draw what you think Mordecai meant when he said this."**

After students have completed their work, allow several of them to share their responses and then ask the following rhetorical questions:

- **Esther was faced with one tough situation. How do you deal with challenging situations?**
- **When your back is up against the wall, do you pout and ask God to take the problem away? Or do you pray, asking God to help you, to teach you and to use you?**

Conclude by asking for commitment: **"God may place you in a tough situation in order to use you. Spend a few minutes talking to God silently about your desire to be available to him, willing to be used by him in any situation."** Remind students that they don't have to go through tough times by themselves. Make yourself and other leaders available to talk through any decisions they need to make.

Close in prayer and distribute copies of **Risky Business**, the mid-week devotional found on page 32, to each student.

Materials needed:
Dry-erase board or chalkboard; marker or chalk; paper; writing utensils; reproducible student sheet on page 32 of this book

Can of Worms!

Each group should have a copy of the following list of questions. Cut each list into strips, and then place the strips in a coffee can or something similar.

Can you recall a time in your life when you got really upset? What did you do?

If you were really upset, how would you want a friend to respond? What would be the worst thing a friend could do?

Have you ever been grounded for something you didn't do? How did you respond?

Have you ever relayed information from one person to another and gotten it wrong? What happened?

HOW DO YOU RESPOND WHEN SOMEONE TELLS YOU THAT YOU CAN'T DO SOMETHING?

SUPPOSE THE PRESIDENT OF THE UNITED STATES CALLED TO GIVE YOU A SPECIAL ASSIGNMENT: WOULD YOU BE EXCITED, SCARED—OR WOULD YOU HANG UP? WHY?

What's one of the most challenging things you've ever done? How did it feel? Were you scared?

Have you ever felt like God wanted you to do something? What was it and what did you do?

Are you someone who can get a tough job done? What's an example of a difficult task you successfully accomplished? If you can't think of a specific tough job you've completed, why should we believe you?

 ©1999 by The Standard Publishing Company. Permission is granted to reproduce this page for ministry purposes only—not for resale.

What's Up With Martin?

A Melodrama

Martin walked slowly along the road, kicking stones as he whistled the "Happy Birthday" song. Suddenly he stopped. He looked around and noticed lots of people were looking back at him. He shyly said, "Hi." And the audience yelled back, "Hi, Martin. You're cool!" Martin blushed with embarrassment and kept walking.

Martin's pager went off. He checked the number and with frustration said, "What now?" As he walked to the nearest payphone, the audience yelled, "Relax, Martin, take it easy." After Martin dialed, he shook his head and made noises that are appropriate during a phone conversation. But suddenly, Martin angrily hung up the phone and kicked the phone booth. Then he went to kick people in the audience, but one person jumped up and said, "Don't mess with us, Martin; we can take ya." Martin fell to his knees and started banging the ground.

Estelle's friends were skipping down the road when one of them asked, "What's with Martin?" Another friend replied, "Let's tell Estelle. She'll know what to do." The last friend picked Martin's pocket, took his money and left the scene to go shopping.

Estelle's friends found Estelle and started talking really fast at the same time so that Estelle had no idea what was going on. So she asked her friend Hank to find out what was happening. While Hank spoke silently with Martin, Estelle's friends finally stopped talking and the audience cheered! Estelle's friends thought *they* were being cheered so they started to talk again, but the audience "booed." Embarrassed, the two friends hid behind Estelle.

Hank returned and told Estelle, "You'll never guess what happened!"

"Tell me," Estelle replied.

"I can't, 'cause you'll never believe me," said Hank.

The audience got impatient. No more than three people started throwing paper wads at the actors. Hank got an attitude and threatened to beat up the audience with one hand tied behind his back. The crowd laughed hysterically until Hank said, "OK, you want to know what happened?"

The crowd cheered!

Hank grabbed a Bible and said, "Read the fourth chapter of Esther," and he walked off the stage.

The crowd shouted, "That's a great idea!" So they read it.

©1999 by The Standard Publishing Company. Permission is granted to reproduce this page for ministry purposes only—not for resale.

RISKY BUSINESS

READ IT
Take some time to reread Esther 4.

THINK ABOUT IT
What did Mordecai mean when he said to Esther, "'And who knows but that you have come to royal position for such a time as this?'"

DO IT
Make a list of all your friends and of every activity you're involved in (school activities, work, hobbies, etc.).

List the ways you have made a positive impact for Christ in the areas you listed above.

List the ways you believe God may want you to make an impact for Christ in these areas.

Ask God to help you accomplish what he wants and then memorize this verse: "'And who knows but that you have come to royal position for such a time as this?'" Esther 4:14

 ©1999 by The Standard Publishing Company. Permission is granted to reproduce this page for ministry purposes only—not for resale.

Truth and Dare 4

Let's face it, living a powerfully bold life for Jesus can be intimidating. Taking a step of faith for him may be the desire of your heart, but not the common sense of your mind! As Christians, we do not have an option about whether or not we walk with God (at least we shouldn't), so what will help us move forward for our Lord? Very simply, knowing the truth. Seeking God and knowing his truth will motivate you to take action—whatever that action means for you. Let's look at Esther, an example of a courageous believer who saved a nation by daring to act on the truth of God!

COUNT THE COST

1 CHAIN REACTION

Separate those students who weren't there last week from those who were. Form groups of five or six students, putting an absent person in each group. (It's OK to have just one group.) Give each group several pieces of tape and jumbled pieces from the reproducible student sheet titled "Chain Reaction."

Begin by saying, **"How many of you have played the game 'Truth or Dare'? Today, we're going to see how Esther dared to live out the truth of God. But to ensure that we all understand the significance of her daring step of faith, I want all of us to do a quick review.**

"I'm handing each group slips of paper that describe events that may or may not have taken place in the book of Esther. You are to tape the correct pieces together to make a chain. Some slips will not be in your chain because they did not happen. You may use your Bibles for help. Once that is done, each person in the group chooses one piece to silently act out for the rest of his group. You have about ten minutes."

(The correct sequence of events is as follows: *1. King Xerxes dismisses Vashti as queen because she wouldn't obey his request. 2. Esther is selected to be the new queen after a long process of*

LESSON TEXT
Esther 4:15–5:8; 7:1-7

LESSON FOCUS
Dare to act on the truth of God, boldly stepping out in faith.

LESSON GOALS
As a result of participating in this lesson, students will:
- Discuss the benefits of taking a step of faith for God.
- Identify the advantages and disadvantages of different options we face as Christians.
- Consider the challenges in living for God and identify solutions.
- Write a personal plan to follow God for the coming week.

Materials needed:
Reproducible student sheet on page 38 of this book; transparent tape for each group

Check This . . .
For the highly motivated (and creative!),
have students act out their section like
characters from their favorite TV shows.
Group members (or the rest of the class)
can guess who the characters are.

beauty treatments. 3. Mordecai saves the king's life by discovering an assassination plot. 4. Haman wants Mordecai and his people to die because Mordecai won't bow down to him. 5. The king unwittingly approves of Haman's plan to kill the Jews. 6. When Mordecai hears about Haman's plan, he weeps and mourns. 7. Mordecai begs Esther to talk to the king. 8. Esther asks the Jewish people to pray for three days before she approaches the king. The other six statements are all devious distractions.)

When the groups complete their reviews, discuss the following:

- **What major decision does Esther face at this moment?**
- **Why is it so difficult to talk to the king?**
- **What kind of person would it take to go ahead with the plan?**

Lead into the next activity by concluding: **"You may not face the same life-or-death choice that Esther did, but I guarantee you'll face choices which require you to exercise faith as you live the Christian life. Let's consider some of those faith-testing choices."**

TAKING THE STEP

Introduce this activity with the following question: **"Would you rather take a step of faith and risk getting hurt (physically or emotionally) or not take a step of faith and live with regret? Why?** (Solicit responses from students.) **Can you think of an example when you did or didn't take that step?"**

After discussing their examples, continue by saying, **"Let's look at a video clip showing someone who risked taking a step of faith. Consider the following questions as you watch."** (Write these questions on the board for easy reference.)

- **What do you think the characters were feeling as they took the step of faith?**
- **Why did they go through with it?**
- **What would be the consequences if they chose not to take this step?**
- **What did they gain?**

In this video clip, Alan Parrish (played by Robin Williams), Judy and Peter attempt to convince Sarah (Alan's old friend) to continue playing "Jumanji" with them. She refuses at first because of the consequences, but then decides to take the risk. The clip begins at 52 minutes, 10 seconds and ends at 55 minutes (it begins at 48 minutes on the longer version).

After the clip has been shown, allow students to respond to the questions on the board.

Wrap up by commenting, **"There are times in life when we're required to take a step of faith. Living the Christian life provides lots of opportunities to exercise our faith. Let's take a look at some ways this is true."**

Materials needed:
TV and VCR; video of *Jumanji*;
chalkboard or dry-erase board; chalk or
marker

Check This . . .
Another video option is *The Sandlot*, a
great video about growing up and friendships. Show the clip toward the end of
the video when "Jet" Rodriguez leaps
over the fence to retrieve the baseball,
even though the "evil monster" is on the
other side of the fence. (This clip begins
at 1 hour, 17 minutes and ends at 1 hour,
20 minutes; it begins at 1 hour, 14 minutes on the longer version.)

GET THE TRUTH

CASE STUDY

You can discuss these case studies as a large group or split up into small groups. Depending on available time, don't feel like you have to do all three case studies. If your time is limited, choose either Case Study 1 or 2 *and* follow up with Case Study 3.

CASE STUDY 1

Big Barrier

It happened again—for the third time this month!

Derrick Stevens, the school's All-State middle linebacker, stuffed your younger brother into a locker and wouldn't let him out until your brother was crying. Now everyone's laughing at your brother and wondering if you're going to do something about it.

The rumor mill says you're afraid to confront Derrick and your brother swears he's never coming back to school.

- **What are your options? (Come up with at least three.)**
- **What are the advantages and disadvantages of each option?**
- **Which option would you choose and why?**

CASE STUDY 2

Planned Parenthood?

Your friend walks up to you, tearfully hands you a note and runs away. You sit down and begin reading,

"Dear Ellen,

You told me to wait, but I didn't. He kept pressuring me and so I let him and now I'm pregnant. Please don't give me any more advice. I just need you to go to the clinic with me next Thursday for my abortion. Will you please come with me?

Promise you won't tell my parents or talk to my boyfriend. Besides, he just broke up with me. If you want to pray, you can. I'm not sure it can hurt at this point. Call me tonight."

- **What are Ellen's options? (Come up with at least three.)**
- **What are your options?**
- **What are the advantages and disadvantages of each option?**
- **Which option would you choose and why?**

CASE STUDY 3

Step of Faith

Read Esther 4.

- **What are Esther's options? (Come up with at least three.)**
- **What are the advantages and disadvantages of each option?**
- **Which option should she choose and why?**

After Case Study 3 is discussed, read Esther 4:15–5:8; 7:1-7 to find out what happened.

Conclude, **"Sometimes we're forced to make tough decisions.**

Materials needed:
Bibles; copies of the case studies

Check This . . .
These case studies can be acted out as role plays if your students prefer dramatization to discussion, although you will want to follow up the case studies with some discussion about the options available in each instance. If you have a large group, divide into six groups and assign the case studies to two groups each.

Doing the right thing is not always easy, which is why it can be a tough decision! Let's consider some of the toughest things we face as Christians."

TURN IT UP!

Introduce this contemporary Christian music activity by saying, **"Taking a step of faith is important. Let's see how that message applies in this song."**

Play song(s) of your choice and then discuss the following questions, which apply to all three songs:

- **What's the message of the chorus?**
- **Do you think that's an important message to succeed as a Christian? In what ways?**
- **What could help Christians actually live the message?**
- **What keeps Christians from living the message?**
- **What's an example of how the message from the chorus can be lived out?**

Comment, **"Now let's return to Esther's story to see whether or not Esther took the step of faith she needed to take."**

Read Esther 4:15–5:8; 7:1-7, then discuss:

- **What was Esther's step of faith?**
- **What would have happened if Esther hadn't dared to take her step of faith?**
- **Did she have any reason to believe she would succeed?**
- **Did she take a blind step of faith or did she prepare before petitioning the king? In what ways?**
- **Would she have made a wrong choice if the king hadn't allowed her to speak? Why?**

Wrap up this activity by saying, **"We've heard a song about daring to live for God, no matter what. Let's consider what your life would be like if you dared to take a step of faith."**

TAKE THE RISK

DARING TO STEP

Begin by stating, **"Living a bold life for Christ can be tough. Turn to the person on your right and think of one or two things you consider to be the hardest things to do as a Christian. When you've got them, come write them on the board."**

Once everyone has participated, the board should be full of responses. Direct students to condense the list to the top five most difficult, and then discuss the following:

- **What's so hard about doing these things?**
- **What can help you to meet these challenges?**
- **Which one of the top five will you dare to do?**
- **Who will hold you accountable?**

Give students a chance to pray together in their pairs for the challenges they've dared to accept.

Materials needed:
CD or cassette player; "My Will," recorded by dc Talk on the *Exodus* release; "Live the Life," by Michael W. Smith, on his album titled *Live the Life*; or "For Such a Time as This," by Wayne Watson, on his *The Way Home* CD; Bibles

Materials needed:
Chalkboard and chalk; or large sheet of butcher paper and marker

2 YOUR SONG

Lead into this activity by saying, **"The chorus of a song is generally repeated several times because it emphasizes the message the singer wants to communicate."** Distribute copies of the reproducible student sheet titled "My Song" on page 39. Then say, **"I want you to write a four- to six-line chorus that communicates your commitment to walk with Christ through a tough situation. Refer to the outline on the student sheet as a guide."**

Give students an opportunity to share their songs (some might want to share next week after they've had more time to think) and close in prayer. Then, distribute copies of **Risky Business**, the midweek devotional found on page 40, as your students depart.

Materials needed:
Reproducible student sheets on pages 39, 40 of this book; writing utensils

Check This:
Play the song "Into Jesus," by dc Talk, recorded on their *Supernatural* CD, as an example of a chorus which communicates commitment to Christ.

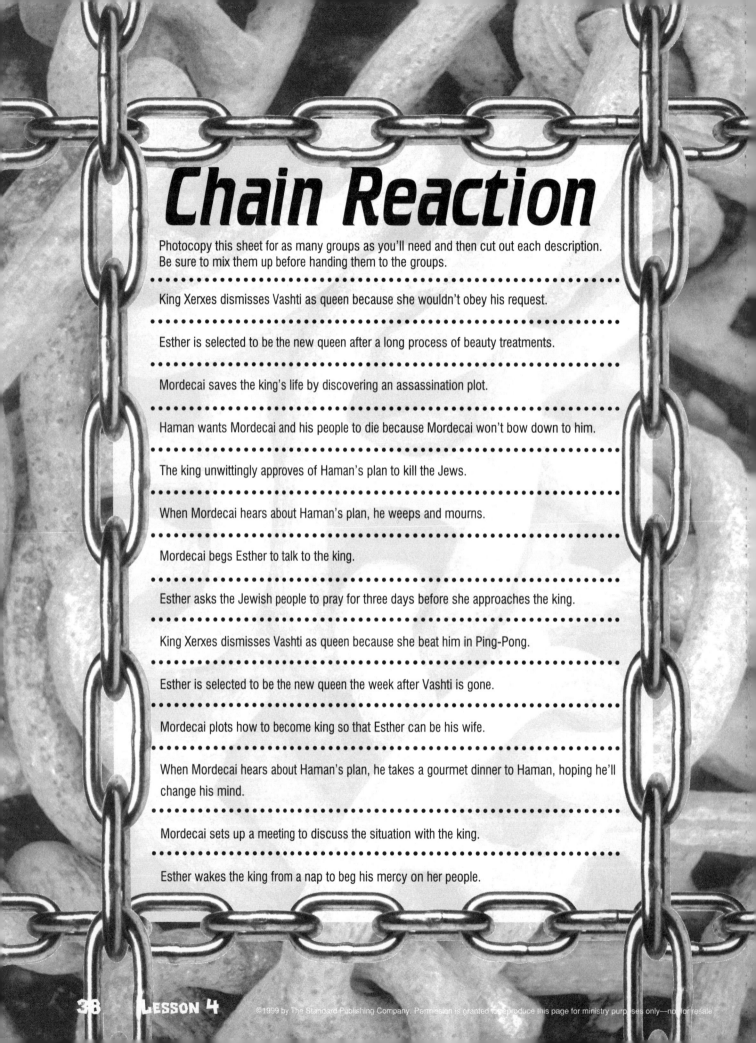

Chain Reaction

Photocopy this sheet for as many groups as you'll need and then cut out each description. Be sure to mix them up before handing them to the groups.

King Xerxes dismisses Vashti as queen because she wouldn't obey his request.

Esther is selected to be the new queen after a long process of beauty treatments.

Mordecai saves the king's life by discovering an assassination plot.

Haman wants Mordecai and his people to die because Mordecai won't bow down to him.

The king unwittingly approves of Haman's plan to kill the Jews.

When Mordecai hears about Haman's plan, he weeps and mourns.

Mordecai begs Esther to talk to the king.

Esther asks the Jewish people to pray for three days before she approaches the king.

King Xerxes dismisses Vashti as queen because she beat him in Ping-Pong.

Esther is selected to be the new queen the week after Vashti is gone.

Mordecai plots how to become king so that Esther can be his wife.

When Mordecai hears about Haman's plan, he takes a gourmet dinner to Haman, hoping he'll change his mind.

Mordecai sets up a meeting to discuss the situation with the king.

Esther wakes the king from a nap to beg his mercy on her people.

©1999 by The Standard Publishing Company. Permission is granted to reproduce this page for ministry purposes only—not for resale

Your Song

The chorus of a song is generally repeated several times because it emphasizes the message the singer wants to communicate.

You have just become a famous songwriter. Your job is to write a lyric of four to six lines that communicates your commitment to walk with Christ through a tough situation. Refer to the following outline as a guide:

A tough situation I am facing is . . .

I believe God wants me to . . .

I've decided I will . . .

I'm going to get help from . . .

My commitment chorus:

©1999 by The Standard Publishing Company. Permission is granted to reproduce this page for ministry purposes only—not for resale.

RISKY BUSINESS

READ IT
Take some time to reread Esther 4:15–5:8; 7:1-7.

THINK ABOUT IT
Be ready for God to lead you to do some great things for him this week. (Remember, a great thing can also be a simple thing. God decides what's great, not us.) Is God daring you to take a step of faith to follow him this week?

DO IT
Keep track of how many times during the week God prompts you to do something (spend time with him, sit with a loner at lunch, etc.), then answer these questions at the end of the week:

Monday

Tuesday

Wednesday

Thursday

Friday

Saturday

• How many of God's promptings did you obey?

• Why did you choose the ones you did?

• Did you trust yourself or God more this week?

• How do you think your week would have been different if you had obeyed God every time?

• What would others say about you?

• What changes would you make for next week?

©1999 by The Standard Publishing Company. Permission is granted to reproduce this page for ministry purposes only—not for resale.

"I Love Me!" 5

All of us suffer from a disease called "selfishness." It rears its ugly head whenever things aren't going our way and often gets us in trouble. There is a cure, but it's expensive. The price? "Don't consider yourself more highly than you ought, but instead consider others better than yourself" (Romans 12:3 and Philippians 2:3, 4).

Once again God has a solution for all of our problems. The challenge, as always, is applying the medicine before we get sick. Haman learns a valuable lesson about selfishness that ends up costing him his life. Will we learn our lesson before the consequences catch up with us?

COUNT THE COST

1 SUPER CELEBRITIES

To begin this session, divide students into two or more teams for a version of "Win, Lose or Draw." The category will be "Celebrities." Students are to think of a famous person they can either pantomime or draw. The celebrities can be either dead or alive. The drawing or action can relate to how the person looks or describe the show, movie, song or accomplishment that he or she is known for.

Teams should take turns acting or drawing while the other team members guess who the celebrity is. Keep score by the amount of celebrities they each guess, and the least amount of time it takes to do so.

After several rounds, declare the winning team and then discuss the following:

- **Of all the celebrities we named, how many of them are known to have an inflated ego?**
- **In what ways are they proud?**
- **Do you care how they act? Do you like when they act proud or does it make you mad? Why?**
- **Do you feel different toward those celebrities who don't act**

LESSON TEXT
Esther 5:9–7:10

LESSON FOCUS
Don't let pride trip you up.

LESSON GOALS
As a result of participating in this lesson, students will:
- Discuss the difference between pride and confidence.
- List the consequences of a proud and selfish lifestyle.
- Illustrate biblical responses to pride and selfishness.
- Analyze their own lives by discussing their habits with friends.

Materials needed:
Chalkboard and chalk; or several sheets of butcher paper with markers; watch with second hand

Check This . . .
While students compete, play the song "Little Man," recorded by the O.C. Supertones on their album *The Supertones Strike Back* or any other song that talks about pride.

egotistically? Why?
- **What's the difference between someone who's proud and someone who's confident?**
- **What's a possible danger to being proud?**

Conclude by saying, "**Pride can get us in trouble. When we're proud, we focus only on ourselves and we become selfish people. Pride is a significant theme in the book of Esther. Let's look at Haman's life and see how he deals with it in his life.**"

LITTLE MAN

Begin this activity by asking students to define "pride" by giving an example. (Get two or three responses.) Then ask:
- **How many of you know someone who is full of pride?**
- **How many of you would admit to being full of pride?**
- **What's so wrong with being proud? How does it affect anyone?**
- **What's the difference between pride and confidence?**

Play the song "Little Man," by the O.C. Supertones. Then discuss the following questions:
- **What would you say are some of the goals of the person they're singing about?**
- **What is unhealthy about these goals?**
- **Do you think this person has friends? If so, describe them. If not, why not?**
- **Is this person's attitude common today? How so?**
- **Do you see yourself in this person? In what way?**

Comment, "**It's one thing to be a confident person. We all should be confident. But pride is another thing. Pride sends the message, 'I'm better than you.' And that's not healthy. Let's jump back into the book of Esther to see the pride issue come alive.**"

Materials needed:
CD or cassette player; CD or cassette of the song "Little Man," recorded by the O.C. Supertones on their album *The Supertones Strike Back*

Check This . . .
For a contrast to a life of pride, play the song "Bowing Down," recorded by Matt Redman on his album *The Friendship and the Fear*.

GET THE TRUTH

CATCH ME—I'M FALLING!

Begin by asking students: "**Who can tell us about a time you said or did something foolish?**" (Get a couple of responses; be ready with your own example.)

Continue by saying, "**We're all guilty of saying or doing things that aren't smart. Right now we're going to focus on one of the main characters in the book of Esther that knows how to be a fool.**"

Put students into groups and give copies of the reproducible student sheet on page 46 to each student. Each group needs about eight to ten items that can be stacked (soda or soup cans work best). Groups can be as small as two people or as large as fifteen. Also, give each group the stackable items. Read the directions together to ensure everyone knows what to do.

After students have completed reading the Scripture and constructing the towers of foolishness, discuss the following:

Materials needed:
Reproducible student sheet on page 46 of this book; writing utensils; numerous items that can be stacked (soda or soup cans work best)

- **How many foolish things did you discover that Haman said or did?**
- **Why were they foolish?**
- **How many still have a tower standing? If it fell, how long did it take to fall? If it's still standing, how steady is it?**
- **What would have kept (or is keeping) the tower from falling over?**
- **How are our foolish decisions in life like your tower?**

Wrap up this activity by saying, **"Haman was a proud man. His pride led him to make many foolish decisions. What about you? How are you doing in the area of pride? Let's do a quick personal checkup."**

HANGMAN

Divide students into small groups of five to six, possibly by letting them choose the boastful celebrity they most despise: Rush Limbaugh, Marilyn Manson, Dennis Rodman, Mike Tyson or Howard Stern. Make sure each group has at least one Bible, something to draw with and a copy of the reproducible student sheet titled "Hangman."

Ask, **"How many of you have played 'Hangman' before? What's the object of the game and what's the penalty if you lose?** (Let a few students respond.) **Imagine if life were really like that! Well, for one person, it was. In your groups, read Esther 5:9–7:10. Each time you think Haman does something that shows pride or selfishness, add a body part on the gallows, such as his head, neck, an arm, hand, leg or foot. We'll see if he ends up hanging himself."**

After the students finish, let them discuss these questions in their groups:

- **How many foolish things did Haman say or do?**
- **Why were they foolish?**
- **How did Haman's pride get him in trouble?**
- **What can we learn from Haman's life?**
- **Are you ever guilty of acting proud? In what ways?**
- **What would you tell a friend who was struggling with pride?**
- **If you were struggling with pride, how would you want someone to tell you?**

Conclude by saying, **"Haman's pride ended up killing him. What is pride doing to you? Let's take a look at some consequences of pride and how we can avoid them."**

Materials needed:
Bibles; reproducible student sheet on page 47 of this book; writing utensils

TAKE THE RISK

1 CREATIVE COVERS

Materials needed:
Paper grocery bags for each student; felt pens or markers; scissors; sample of a completed book cover

Begin by saying, **"Think about your life for a moment. What are some areas you would agree you need to be less selfish in? Are there other areas where you're too full of pride? If you're not sure, let's look at some Bible verses which might help bring something to mind:"**

• **Romans 12:3:** "For by the grace given me I say to every one of you: Do not think of yourself more highly than you ought, but rather think of yourself with sober judgment, in accordance with the measure of faith God has given you."

• **Philippians 2:3, 4:** "Do nothing out of selfish ambition or vain conceit, but in humility consider others better than yourselves. Each of you should look not only to your own interests, but also to the interests of others."

Ask students to **"Sum up either of these verses in five words or less."** (Give students some time to think.) Then continue by asking, **"What would that phrase look like illustrated?"**

Say, **"I'm going to give you a chance to show me. Let's use our illustrations and phrases to design a book cover that can serve as a permanent reminder for each of us. It can be used at home or school to warn us of the dangers of selfishness and the responsibility we have to put others first."**

Distribute the materials to students and give them time to work. After 10 to 15 minutes, encourage them to share their completed projects.

2 WORD PICTURES

Materials needed:
Paper; drawing utensils

Check This . . .
While students work, play the song "Dear Heavenly," recorded by Fade from their album *The Debut*. It's a song that reminds us that life is empty without God.

Comment, **"Haman's pride cost him his life. That may not happen to you, but what are some other possible consequences to pride and selfishness?"** (Solicit student responses.)

Read Romans 12:3 and Philippians 2:3, 4 and then ask students, **"What do these verses teach and how can they help us deal with pride in our lives?"**

Continue by saying, **"Each person should choose one idea from these verses to illustrate. What can you draw to help you remember what you should do (or not do), according to what the verse teaches?"**

Distribute the paper and drawing utensils. Allow students about 10 minutes to complete their illustrations. When they have completed their work, encourage them to explain their pictures in the groups from the previous activity. Direct students to share one way their group can pray for them in the coming week.

3 TWO FER ONE

Materials needed:
Paper; writing utensils; reproducible student sheet on page 48 of this book

Comment, **"Pride is costly and can have negative consequences, both long-term and short-term. So we need a plan to help reduce the lingering effects of those consequences.**

What's the best plan? Don't be guilty of pride! Before we discuss how that will work, you need to do the following: Get in groups of two to four and make sure you know each other's names and phone numbers."

Direct students into small groups and distribute the paper and writing utensils, then continue by saying, **"Now that you are in groups, each of you will make up a silly rule for your group, such as 'no one can speak by moving his lips.' Along with the rule, each of you has to come up with two fun consequences if the rule is broken, such as 'you must bow in front of the teacher and then hug everyone in one of the other groups.' So, in reality you get 'two fer one.'"**

Allow students the necessary time to come up with their rules and consequences. After everyone has had a chance to create the rules for their group, share the following: **"Now, as a group brainstorm 10 possible penalties for your group if any of you is guilty of being proud during the next week. Agree to call one another at least once this week to see how you're doing and to pray for one another. Then, next week if there are any guilty parties, you will have to perform two of the 10 penalties in front of everyone. (The penalty will be selected by your group members.)"**

In your groups pray for God's help to be less proud during the coming week. Then distribute copies of **Risky Business**, the mid-week devotional found on page 48, to each student.

Catch Me I'm Falling!

Read the following sections from Esther. After each section, write down and number each thing that Haman says or does that you consider foolish. Indicate why you consider it foolish.

For each foolish word or act, stack one of the items your group received on top of the other as you build a tower of foolishness.

Section 1:
Esther 5:9-14

Section 2:
Esther 6:1-14

Section 3:
Esther 7:1-10

 ©1999 by The Standard Publishing Company. Permission is granted to reproduce this page for ministry purposes only—not for resale.

Hangman

Did you ever play "Hangman" as a kid? What's the object of the game and what's the penalty if you lose? Imagine if life were really like that!

Read Esther 5:9–7:10. Each time you think Haman does something that shows pride or selfishness, place a body part on the gallows. We'll see if he ends up hanging himself.

• How many foolish things did Haman say or do?

• Why were they foolish?

• How did Haman's pride get him in trouble?

• What can we learn from Haman's life?

• Are you ever guilty of acting proud? In what ways?

• What would you tell a friend who was struggling with pride?

• If you were struggling with pride, how would you want someone to tell you?

©1999 by The Standard Publishing Company. Permission is granted to reproduce this page for ministry purposes only—not for resale.

RISKY BUSINESS

READ IT
Take some time to reread Esther 5:9–7:10.

THINK ABOUT IT
Write down what lessons you've learned from Haman's life.

What do you think is a correct, biblical way to act toward those who are selfish and proud?

DO IT
If people told you that they thought you were selfish and proud, how would you respond? (Write out your plan.)

Ask one or two friends to give you honest feedback to the following questions:
- When have you seen me act selfishly?
- Do I talk about myself too much?
- Am I a good listener?
- Am I encouraging?
- What can I do to improve in any of these areas?

THINK ABOUT IT
What have you learned about the hazards of pride and what are you going to do about it?

DO IT
Spend some time in prayer, asking God to show you what to do.

©1999 by The Standard Publishing Company. Permission is granted to reproduce this page for ministry purposes only—not for resale.

Power Surge 6

Help! Have you ever felt like your back was against the wall and you had nowhere to go? What did you do? To whom did you turn? When you're desperate, any remedy looks good. Most remedies last for only a short while, but when you want a real solution, God is the One to turn to.

Esther and Mordecai faced a huge dilemma: their people, the Jews, were to be destroyed in less than a year. They now had the king as their ally, but he had previously set into motion a law that permitted the attack on the Jews, and according to the laws of the Medes and Persians, the law couldn't be reversed. King Xerxes gave Mordecai permission to do whatever he thought best, and so God granted Mordecai the wisdom to know how to deal with the situation.

What happened? The Jewish people were delivered from their enemies. We can learn valuable lessons about God's faithfulness as well as important considerations when fighting in a hostile environment.

COUNT THE COST

1 HOLLYWOOD'S GREATEST RESCUES

Begin this activity by saying, **"There are innumerable TV shows today that deal with real-life drama and amazing rescues. But none beat the action, suspense and intensity of Secret Agent James Bond. Let's watch a clip of one of Bond's nail-biting escapes from one of the 007 movies."**

Every James Bond film begins with some hair-raising incident of adventure, escape and deliverance. Pick one you deem appropriate. Then discuss the following:

- **What was going on? Recap the events.**
- **What helped Bond complete his task?**
- **What would you have done differently?**

LESSON TEXT
Esther 8–10

LESSON FOCUS
In the midst of difficult situations, turn to God for protection.

LESSON GOALS
As a result of participating in this lesson, students will:

- Consider how and when God has rescued them.
- Discuss the theological tension that exists between God being all-powerful yet allowing "bad" things to happen.
- Realize that Christians need to understand how their world operates in order to be positive change agents.
- Commit to living a healthy Christian life so that they'll be able to make a difference for God.

Materials needed:
TV and VCR; videotape of any James Bond movie (The Indiana Jones series or other action-packed movies of this genre would work equally well.)

- Tell us about a situation when you had to be rescued or when you did the rescuing. How did it feel to be rescued or to do the rescuing?
- Do you ever feel like God has rescued you? What happened?
- How effective do you think James Bond would be in fighting modern-day evils such as pornography or abortion?

Conclude by saying, **"When James Bond fights his enemies, he has the latest technological gadgets to give him the edge (not to mention the fact that the action is scripted!). But Secret Agent 007 can't help us. In real life, we need someone to deliver us from problems, someone to help us think through issues from a Christian perspective. Let's continue in our study of Esther to see what insight we can gain."**

CAPTURE THE EGG

If you do not have a large room for this activity, you may want to go outside for this game. Comment, **"This** (hold the egg or tennis ball) **is your teammate. Your teammate has been kidnapped through the other team's devious plotting and needs to be rescued. Only you can do it, but the other team awaits you. Beware or you will become like this egg, forever trapped and waiting to be rescued!"**

This game is based on "Capture the Flag," but you use eggs instead of flags. Eggs? Yes! Split your students into two teams and put one egg in each team's protected area. The goal is to cross enemy lines, retrieve the egg and bring it to your side without getting touched. However, the egg may be passed, tossed or thrown to another teammate. Of course there are consequences to doing it that way. (That's why you have a dozen eggs available.) If eggs won't work for your setting, tennis balls work just as well!

After a couple of rounds (or as time allows), discuss the following:

- **What emotions did you feel as you tried to rescue your egg?**
- **Did your team have any kind of strategy as you played, or was it every person for himself or herself?**
- **Have you ever been rescued or saved by someone? (It doesn't have to be a life-or-death story.)**
- **Have you ever rescued someone from something, whether from making a bad mistake or from getting hurt in some way?**
- **What did you feel like in those times of rescue?**
- **Do you ever feel like God has rescued you? How?**

Conclude by saying, **"The truth is, God has rescued all of**

Materials needed:
Cones or markers; a dozen eggs (You can substitute tennis balls if the eggs don't work in your setting!); damp towels (for any necessary cleanup!)

Check This . . .
While students are playing the game, play the soundtrack from a James Bond, Indiana Jones or other action film.

us in one way or another. Often we don't see God at work, but he is protecting us in all things and at all times. Let's see how God provided for and protected Esther and the Jewish people as we conclude our study on the book of Esther."

GET THE TRUTH

TRUE OR FALSE?

To begin this activity, say something like this: **"All of us have a view of God. Let's discuss our view of God's presence in our lives. True or False?:"**

- **God is in control of all circumstances and situations.**
- **God protects his children.**
- **God is with us at all times.**
- **God can bring good out of all situations.**
- **God is with a 13-year-old girl on her birthday.**
- **God is with that same girl when she scores the winning basket.**
- **God is with the same girl if she misses the winning basket.**
- **God is with the same girl if she gets raped after the game.**

Discuss their thoughts on the above. After a while, ask this follow-up question: **"What good can possibly come out of a teenage girl getting raped?"**

Read aloud Esther 8:1, 2.

- **King Xerxes just gave Mordecai a significant position of influence. Could God have allowed that to happen in order to protect the Jews? How?** (God allowed two Jewish people to rise to the top of authority in the kingdom.)

Read aloud Esther 8:3-8.

- **Why couldn't the king just revoke his former law?** (See the end of verse 8.)
- **What did the king give Mordecai permission to do?** (Write a new law.)

Read aloud Esther 8:9-11.

- **What did the new law allow?** (It allowed the Jews to fight back.)

Read aloud Esther 9:1-3.

- **What is the attitude of the people toward the Jews?** (Verses 2 and 3 show that the people were afraid of the Jews.)
- **Why do you think they were afraid?** (Three possible reasons: Not only were Esther and Mordecai in power, but now the king was sympathetic toward the Jews; the Jews were able to defend themselves; they remembered what had happened to Haman when he attacked the Jews.)
- **How do these things show God's control and protection?**

Materials needed:
Bibles

Check This . . .
This is a pretty heavy topic. Be ready to give examples of how God is in control, even when things seem out of control.

Check This . . .
For another example of a time when God was at work even in the midst of a chaotic situation, read *The Hiding Place*, by Corrie Ten Boom and discover why Corrie and Betsie thank God for the fleas in their barracks. (Read chapter 13 and the first couple of pages of chapter 14 for the context, then use the sections that are most pertinent.)

Read aloud Esther 9:5 to show what happened.

Wrap up this activity by saying, **"When crazy situations or even tragedies happen in life, we can ask one of two questions: Where's God? Or, How is God going to use this? The second question isn't an easy one, but it shows we know how to trust him during confusing times."**

ACTION NEWS

Prior to the lesson, take a student (or assign this as a project for a few) with you to a popular spot and videotape responses to the following question: *"What is a significant issue in today's society that needs to be fixed? Why is this so important?"* Delete responses that make the tape too long.

Begin this activity by saying, **"Esther and Mordecai need a miracle. They and the rest of the Jews are going to be destroyed unless God intervenes. Let's see what happens."**

Read aloud Esther 8:1-8.

• **What's happening in this section?**

Read aloud Esther 8:9-14.

• **What does Mordecai do?**

Read aloud Esther 9:1-5.

• **What was the result?**

Comment, **"God allowed Mordecai to be a national leader, but that didn't solve the problem. Because of the king's previous law, Mordecai had to come up with a plan that would counter that law. Mordecai was able to do so because he understood the law and how it worked. He responded to a current situation with wisdom and used the position God had given him to help save his people.**

"Mordecai was a wise man, and that's what we need to be as Christians. God allows each of us to have certain friendships or positions in school, on a team or in the community that can influence others. But we need to be 'as shrewd as snakes and as innocent as doves' (Matthew 10:16). Let's look at some issues in today's society that Christians need to address."

List the issues on the board as they are addressed on tape. After watching the tape, direct students to form small groups of four or five and say, **"In your small group, pick one of the issues introduced on the tape. Discuss appropriate ways Christians ought to respond to that issue, and then come up with the perfect plan to do so."**

Allow about five minutes for small-group discussion, then ask the groups to summarize their conclusions. Discuss these responses.

Conclude: **"As Christians, we have a responsibility to proclaim God's truth in our communities. But no change is as important as making sure our own hearts and lives are**

Materials needed:
Prepared videotape; TV and VCR; paper; writing utensils; chalkboard or dry-erase board; chalk or marker

Check This . . .
Be sure to ask permission before you attempt to interview people on tape! Official IDs, such as a church business card, might be beneficial, if someone asks to see any identification. Respecting people's "No"s is important too.

right with God. Before we try to change the world, let's be sure we're looking at our own lives and taking care of first things first."

TAKE THE RISK

1 POWERFUL PROTECTOR

Comment, **"Life does not always make sense. In fact, it's often confusing, especially when the Bible teaches that God is always with us and is all-powerful. Since that's so, it seems like God would take away a lot of our pain, but he doesn't, so he must have some reasons."**

Form groups of four to eight students, possibly by allowing them to choose their favorite "superhero" (Superman, Batman, Spiderman, Wonder Woman, the Incredible Hulk, etc.). Distribute copies of the reproducible student sheet titled "Powerful Protector" to each student and give them about 10 minutes to complete the sheet.

After all groups are done, discuss the results together as a large group. Then close by reading 2 Corinthians 1:3, 4: "Praise be to the God and Father of our Lord Jesus Christ, the Father of compassion and the God of all comfort, who comforts us in all our troubles, so that we can comfort those in any trouble with the comfort we ourselves have received from God."

Materials needed:
Reproducible student sheet on page 54 of this book; writing utensils

Check This . . .
Discuss the subject of God's presence in our lives after listening to "Consume Me," from dc Talk's *Supernatural* CD, or check out "To Say Thanks," by Nichole Nordeman, recorded on her debut release titled *Wide Eyed*.

2 BRAINSTORM

Distribute the reproducible student sheet titled "Brainstorm" on page 55 to each student. They should work in groups of four to eight students for the first section and individually for the second section. At the end of today's session, be sure to invite students to talk to you or other leaders for additional support on anything they wrote down.

Close in prayer, then distribute copies of **Risky Business**, the midweek devotional found on page 56, as your students depart.

Materials needed:
Reproducible student sheets on pages 55, 56 of this book; writing utensils

POWERFUL
protector

"Where's God?"

That's a common cry when people are struggling, and it's also a fair question. It's hard to understand what God is doing during tough times. But he is always doing something. Discuss the following:

• As a group, come up with five or six situations you've experienced (or that you've made up) that were/are hard to understand (for example: a friend gets cancer, you break your leg before the big game, lose your voice the night of the play, etc.).

• In what ways could God have protected you from additional harm? What could God have been teaching you?

• What did you learn about God during your tough times?

 ©1999 by The Standard Publishing Company. Permission is granted to reproduce this page for ministry purposes only—not for resale.

BRAINSTORM

PaRt One

Make a list of five to seven specific areas of life that teens struggle with today.

1.

2.

3.

4.

5.

6.

7.

Pick two of the above and write a plan that would help a student be victorious in those areas. Consider what outside help they might need and what specific action steps they should take.

1.

2.

ParT TwO

What about you? Is there anything from this list that you struggle with? Is there another issue that needs to be addressed in your life?

What steps can you take this week that will help you be victorious?

©1999 by The Standard Publishing Company. Permission is granted to reproduce this page for ministry purposes only—not for resale.

RISKY BUSINESS

READ IT

Take some time to reread Esther 8–10.

THINK ABOUT IT

Communication is so important in a healthy relationship. Sometimes when we get frustrated or confused about circumstances in our friendships, we pretend the difficulties don't bother us and ignore them, hoping they'll go away. The questions seldom do; instead, they usually grow and come back to bite us.

That can be true in our relationship with God, too. Have you ever been frustrated about how God handled a situation in your life or someone else's life? Take some time this week to reflect on that. Write down any questions you've always wanted to ask God.

DO IT

Spend some time writing a letter to God. Talk to him about your questions, but also take time to listen. Spend some time in his Word and see what he has to say to you.

©1999 by The Standard Publishing Company. Permission is granted to reproduce this page for ministry purposes only—not for resale.

Think about it! God has done so much for each of us, yet rarely do we celebrate his goodness and share with one another how thankful we are to have such a great God. That's exactly why the Feast of Purim (pronounced poo-REEM) was established. Mordecai wanted the Jews to remember what God had done and then to show their thankfulness by expressing God's love to others. What a terrific example for all of us as believers! We are to celebrate God's love and protection and then demonstrate his love to those around us through service. The Feast of Purim is traditionally celebrated early in the springtime, but *any* time of the year is right for a praise party.

PROCLAMATION

Several weeks in advance, inform students that you will be having a Praise Party based on the principles behind the Feast of Purim: remembrance of God's protection, celebration of his love with food and fun and expression of gratitude by serving others.

PREPARATION

Read Esther 9:20-22 which explains the origins of the Feast of Purim and then explain that the Praise Party will give them the opportunity to praise God, party and participate in service. Outline the tasks of the three praise teams indicated below and allow students to go to the one of their preference (with the provision that you might have to recruit "volunteers" if the groups are too uneven).

THE "THANK GOD!" PRAISE TEAM

These students will spearhead the praise and thanksgiving time. Several suggested activities are listed below in the *Remembrance* section but encourage them to brainstorm other ideas for the group to express its gratitude for God's love and protection. Emphasize to them that the thanksgiving and remembrance time will set the tone for the Praise Party.

TEXT
Esther 9:18-32

FOCUS
This special event will adopt the celebratory thanksgiving spirit the Jews commemorate annually on the Feast of Purim. The Praise Party will encourage your students to:
- Remember what God has done and how he has rescued them in their lives.
- Share with God and others their thankfulness for what God has done.
- Celebrate God's goodness.
- Show God's love to others by doing a service project.

Check This . . .
A resource that provides some excellent background information on the Feast of Purim is *Handbook of Bible Festivals*, by Galen Peterson (order #3088 from Standard Publishing at 1-800-543-1353). This book deals with the biblical heritage, modern observance and contemporary application of the Feast of Purim. And, it includes a great recipe for a Jewish pastry!

THE "LET'S PARTY!" PRAISE TEAM

Every party needs organizers who take care of the details: food, drinks and all the serving utensils; decorations which reflect the praise theme; and music. (What's a party without music?) Allow students to be creative while providing any needed support and oversight. Remind them that cleanup time can also be a time of praise and service. These students are not *solely* responsible for providing the food or cleaning up; they are organizing all the details and recruiting the volunteers.

THE "HELPING HANDS" PRAISE TEAM

Mordecai included "gifts to the poor" in his proclamation of the first Purim celebration, and God repeatedly reminds us to live out our faith. Instruct this group of students to determine one or two service projects which the whole group can perform as part of the Praise Party. You can offer suggestions that you think are appropriate, but leave the final choice up to the students.

Service opportunities are limitless. Your church office may know of church families in need. Local Christian agencies, homeless shelters or convalescent centers will also offer options for service. You will need to provide guidance in lining up the date, transportation, additional adult chaperones and necessary supplies. You will also need to help in securing the approval of both the parents and the group(s) being assisted, but allow the students to participate. And remind them that the party doesn't end once they start helping others. Their gratitude attitudes should go with them!

CELEBRATION

A. REMEMBRANCE

The Praise Party should begin with the remembrance of "when their sorrow was turned into joy and their mourning into a day of celebration" (Esther 9:22). Allow the "Thank God!" Praise Team to lead during this time. They can use some of the activities listed below and/or create their own:

GOD'S WORK OF ART

Materials needed:
Butcher paper; markers; masking tape

Form groups of five or six. Direct one person from each group to lie down on a piece of butcher paper and another to trace his or her body outline onto the paper. Once the outlines are complete, tape the posters where all the groups can see them as they discuss the following:

- **What were some tough things you went through this last year?**
- **What did God teach you through them?**
- **What part of you did God protect? (Depressed? Maybe God protected your mind by helping you think right thoughts. Fight with a friend? Maybe God protected your mouth by helping you say right words. Got caught shoplifting? Maybe God pro-**

tected your hands by helping you not steal anything else.)

When groups are done, have them go to their outlines to write a word of love or draw a picture of thanks on the part of the body that God protected.

DOWN MEMORY LANE

Read Esther 9:18-32 to remind students of the origin of the Feast of Purim. The name *purim* is a plural Hebrew word meaning "lots." The name is taken from the lots that were used by Haman to ascertain the date for the destruction of the Jews, a common practice among cultures of the ancient Near East for determining divine will. In commemoration of this day that was slated for defeat but became a victory, Mordecai and Esther decreed that all Jews should celebrate Purim on an annual basis. Remind students how God was faithful to Israel.

Then break into groups of four or five to give all participants a chance to share their praises in front of others and periodically take time to clap and cheer for what God has done.

Be sure to take time to sing songs of praise and to pray prayers of thanks. It would be helpful if one member of the "Thank God!" Praise Team participated in each of the small groups.

When all the groups have shared, spend some more time in prayer and in song.

Materials needed:
Bibles; CD player and CDs

Check This . . .
Some CDs that would be great for this time of group worship include *Exodus* (Rocketown Records); *Nitro Praise* (N Soul); *Petra Praise 2: We Need Jesus* (Word); and the CD packaged with the Psalms study titled *Heart Burn: Blazing Hot Worship* (Standard Publishing).

A ROUND OF APPLAUSE

This activity can be done either in small groups during the *Remembrance* time or later. Part of the Purim festival is "giving presents . . . to one another" (Esther 9:22). Students can do this by sharing words of gratitude with at least three people in the group of how God has used these people to encourage them in their Christian walk.

Check This . . .
For the truly creative, make small gift cards which everyone can use to write notes to one another.

NOW, A WORD FROM OUR SPONSOR . . .

Record video interviews with the ministers, church leaders and others about how God has faithfully protected them over the past year. Then show the tape during the party. Find people who have faced difficult challenges such as unemployment, serious illness or family struggles and who are willing to share their testimony of God's provision through adversity.

Materials needed:
Video camera; videotape; VCR

B. LET'S PARTY!

Now it's time for the "Let's Party!" Praise Team to take over. This celebration time may occur right after the *Remembrance* portion or after the service project, depending on the project you select and the time of day.

Materials needed:
Food; drinks; party supplies; CD player and CDs

C. HIT THE ROAD

Follow through on what the "Helping Hands" Praise Team has planned for the group. Matthew 6:1-4 is an excellent passage of Scripture to read concerning motivation for service. Talk about earthly and heavenly rewards for serving. As students head off to serve, remind them that they should do everything "in the name of the Lord Jesus, giving thanks to God the Father through him" (Colossians 3:17).

NOTES

INTRODUCTION

[1]Charles Swindoll, *Esther* (Nashville, TN: Word Publishing, 1997), p. x. Used by permission.

Other EMPOWERED™ YOUTH PRODUCTS from Standard Publishing

order # 23315
(ISBN 0-7847-1099-6)

WHAT'S THE BIG DEAL ABOUT SEX?

By Jim Burgen

In a national survey of teens, 99% said their number-one concern is how to say no to sexual pressure. Did you know:

- AIDS has been the sixth leading cause of death among 15-24 year olds since 1991?
- Every day 2,700 teens become pregnant?
- Every 24 hours, another 3,000 lose their virginity?
- Of those that become pregnant, more than three in ten choose to abort the baby?

But God has a better way. The *big deal* is that God has an awesome plan for this generation. In a direct, humorous and compelling way the author gives real answers to questions about waiting, dating, homosexuality, interracial dating, dealing with mistakes and more. And each chapter gives readers an opportunity to get personal with questions for reflection. Whether you work with junior-high or senior-high teens, this book will help you deal with this hot topic in a relevant way.

order # 23312
(ISBN 0-7847-0762-6)

ALIEN INVASION A Creative Study of the Book of Ephesians

By Michael Warden

This six-session elective for junior- and senior-high teens will help your students understand their new identity in Christ and launch a fresh invasion in their own lives. Each session features reproducible student sheets, contemporary Christian music suggestions, a midweek guide for personal devotions and numerous options! Also includes a bonus event that will let students spread God's Word to others in a strategic way.

FREESTYLIN' A Creative Study of the Book of Galatians

By Bryan Belknap

This six-session resource for junior- and senior-high teens will help your students discover the freedom they have in Christ. This course emphasizes the ability to live by faith, free from sin and fear of the Law. Each session features video clip and music suggestions, reproducible student sheets, a midweek guide for personal devotions and creative learning activities! Also features a bonus outreach game that provides students an opportunity to make real-life application.

order # 23313
(ISBN 0-7847-0903-3)

order # 23318
(ISBN 0-7847-0952-1)

WHAT'S YOUR POINT? A Creative Study of the Book of Colossians

By Michael Warden

This six-session elective for junior- and senior-high teens will help them focus not on things that don't really matter, but on the true point of life—following Jesus. Each session features reproducible student sheets, suggestions for using contemporary Christian music, a midweek guide for personal devotions and numerous options! A bonus project gives students an opportunity to demonstrate their devotion to Christ in some practical ways.

HEARTBURN A Blazing Six-Week Study of the Psalms

By Rick Bundschuh

Psalm 39:3 says, "My heart grew hot within me, and as I meditated, the fire burned." This six-session resource will set senior-high teens ablaze by exploring the breadth and width of God-centered worship. The package comes complete with a CD featuring red-hot modern Christian music by bands like Spooky Tuesday, Havalina Rail Co., 180 and Soul-Junk. In addition to chord and lyric sheets for all six worship tunes, additional pages feature band photos and bios, thoughts on contemporary worship, reproducible student sheets and a guide for personal devotions.

coming soon!

order # 23316
(ISBN 0-7847-0930-0)

TO ORDER, CONTACT YOUR LOCAL CHRISTIAN BOOKSTORE.

(IF THE BOOK IS OUT OF STOCK, YOU CAN ORDER BY CALLING 1-800-543-1353.)